Baby first arink

Story by Beverley Randell

Illustrated by Ernst Papps

Spring is here.

Baby Lamb is here.

Baby Lamb is hungry.
"Baa-baa. Baa-baa."

Mother Sheep is here.
"Here I am,
Baby Lamb."

Baby Lamb is up.
Baby Lamb is looking for milk.
"Baa-baa. Baa-baa."

Here is the milk.

Here is the milk

for Baby Lamb.

Look at Baby Lamb's tail!

Mother Sheep
and Baby Lamb
are happy in the spring.

16